Follow That Food Chain

A Savanna Food Chain

A WHO-EATS-WHAT
Adventure in Africa

Rebecca Hogue Wojahn   Donald Wojahn

Lerner Publications Company
Minneapolis

For Eli and Cal. We hope this answers some of your questions.

There are many links in the chain that created this series. Thanks to Laura Waxman, Carol Hinz, Kitty Creswell, Danielle Carnito, Sarah Olmanson, Paul Rodeen, the staff of the L.E. Phillips Memorial Public Library, and finally, Katherine Hogue

Lerner Publications Company
A division of Lerner Publishing Group, Inc.
241 First Avenue North
Minneapolis, MN 55401 U.S.A.

Website address: www.lernerbooks.com

Library of Congress Cataloging-in-Publication Data

Wojahn, Rebecca Hogue.
    A savanna food chain : a who-eats-what adventure in Africa / by Rebecca Hogue Wojahn and Donald Wojahn.
        p.   cm. — (Follow that food chain)
    Includes bibliographical references and index.
    ISBN 978–0–8225–7498–9 (lib. bdg. : alk. paper)
    1. Savanna ecology—Africa—Juvenile literature. 2. Food chains (Ecology)—Juvenile literature. I. Wojahn, Donald. II. Title.
QH194.W65 2009
577.4'8096—dc22   2008022889

Manufactured in the United States of America
1 2 3 4 5 6 – BP – 14 13 12 11 10 09

Contents

Introduction
WELCOME TO THE SAVANNA

The sky seems extra big out on the African savanna. That's because it's tall grass and thorny bushes for as far as you can see. Trees scattered here and there offer a bit of shade. Every so often, cliffs or stony hills called **kopjes** rise out of the flat earth.

Here on the savanna, you'll find some of the fastest, fiercest, biggest, and most beautiful animals on the planet. Tucked away in all that grass are stalking lions, screaming baboons, racing cheetahs, and enormous elephants.

The savanna stretches across nearly half of Africa. But these wide grasslands are far from endless. Farmers are using more and more of the space on the savanna to raise cattle. The farms divide the land and destroy the grass. Floods and **drought** threaten to change the land even more. But people throughout Africa are working to protect the savanna. After all, this rich **habitat** is home to thousands of **species** of animals. Come meet a few of them in this book.

4

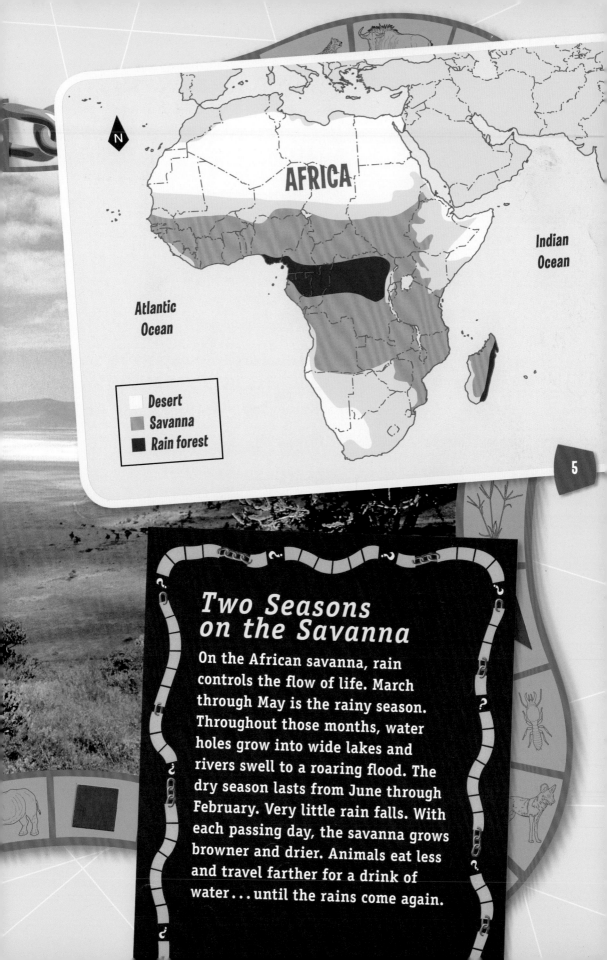

AFRICA

N

Atlantic
Ocean

Indian
Ocean

Desert
Savanna
Rain forest

Two Seasons on the Savanna

On the African savanna, rain controls the flow of life. March through May is the rainy season. Throughout those months, water holes grow into wide lakes and rivers swell to a roaring flood. The dry season lasts from June through February. Very little rain falls. With each passing day, the savanna grows browner and drier. Animals eat less and travel farther for a drink of water...until the rains come again.

Choose a
TERTIARY CONSUMER

All the living things in the savanna are necessary for its health and survival. From the Bermuda grass under your shoes to the spotted hyena lurking up ahead, the living things are all connected. Animals and other organisms feed on and transfer energy to one another. This is called a **food chain** or a **food web**.

In food chains, the strongest **predators** are called **tertiary consumers**. They hunt other animals for food and have few natural enemies. Some of the animals they eat are called **secondary consumers**. Secondary consumers are also predators. They hunt plant-eating animals. Plant eaters are **primary consumers**.

Plants are **producers**. Using energy from the sun, they produce their own food. Plants take in **nutrients** from the soil. They also provide nutrients to the animals that eat them.

Decomposers are insects or **bacteria** that break down dead plants and animals. Decomposers change them into the nutrients found in the soil.

The plants and animals in a food chain depend on one another. Sometimes there's a break in the chain, such as one type of animal dying out. This loss ripples through the rest of the habitat.

Begin your journey through the savanna food web by choosing a tertiary consumer. These **carnivores**, or meat eaters, are at the top of the food chain. That means, for the most part, they don't have any enemies on the savanna (except for humans).

When it's time for the tertiary consumer to eat, pick its meal and flip to that page. As you go through the book, don't be surprised if you backtrack and end up where you never expected to be. That's how food webs work—they're complicated. And watch out for those dead ends! When you hit one of those, you have to go back to page 7 and start over with another tertiary consumer.

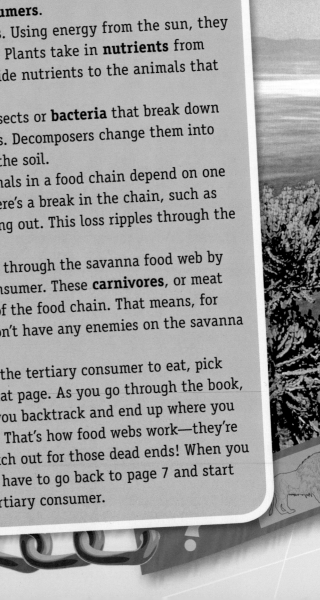

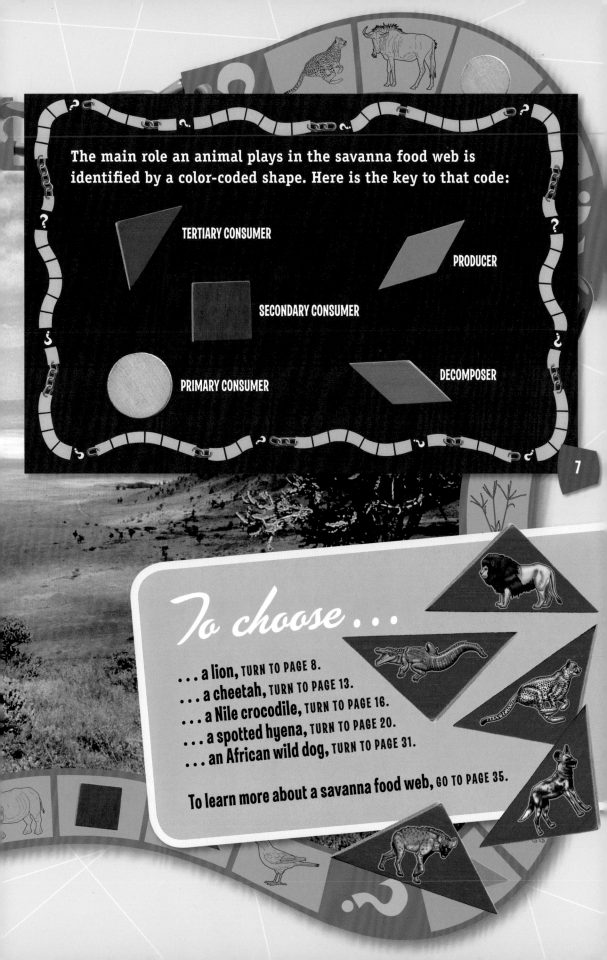

The main role an animal plays in the savanna food web is identified by a color-coded shape. Here is the key to that code:

TERTIARY CONSUMER

PRODUCER

SECONDARY CONSUMER

PRIMARY CONSUMER

DECOMPOSER

To choose . . .

. . . a lion, TURN TO PAGE 8.

. . . a cheetah, TURN TO PAGE 13.

. . . a Nile crocodile, TURN TO PAGE 16.

. . . a spotted hyena, TURN TO PAGE 20.

. . . an African wild dog, TURN TO PAGE 31.

To learn more about a savanna food web, GO TO PAGE 35.

LION (Panthera leo)

As the day grows dim, a roar echoes for miles across the savanna. The lion is waking up. He yawns wide. But he's not tired. After all, he's slept more than twenty hours today. Yawning is simply part of his getting-up ritual. His giant yawn shows off his 2.5-inch (6.4-centimeter) teeth.

Beside him, the females start stirring. It's almost time for them to begin their nightly hunt. The male lion roars again. He's the leader of his pride, or family group. And he's making sure that any lion within earshot knows that this is his pride's territory. His pride has six females, their cubs, and two young males. Lions are unusual that way. They are the only big cats that live and hunt together in groups.

The lion won't hunt with the lionesses tonight. It's their job to bring home dinner and tend to the cubs. His job is to protect the pride. From the kopje, he watches the females move silently out into the night. While he waits, he urinates on his back paws and uses them to scratch deep in the dirt. He's spreading his scent around to mark his territory. When other lions smell it, they'll know to stay away.

A male lion first grows his mane when he's about two years old. (That's about when he's first able to roar too.) But the color of his mane can be a surprise. Manes are sometimes pale blond, brown, or almost black. Scientists have found that female lions prefer lions with darker manes. But they aren't sure why.

Meanwhile, the lionesses stalk a nearby herd of wildebeests. They have picked out a straggler. They crouch, creep ... and pounce. But the wildebeest gets away. The lionesses come up empty. Still hungry, they circle around the herd again.

Lions are surprisingly unsuccessful hunters. In fact, their **prey** gets away more often than it's caught. But the cats get lucky with their second attack. Together they kill a wildebeest. It sprawls dead on the ground.

With a growl, the male lion approaches to eat. The females step aside without complaining. They wait while he tears into the wildebeest. As the pride's leader, he always eats first. Soon the other males join in too. And in times when food is scarce? Well, it's just too bad if there isn't enough for the females and their cubs.

The lion pins the wildebeest down with his paws and tears off a bite of food. A three-year-old cub mews and creeps forward. With a snarl, the older lion spins and swats the cub with a massive paw. The cub doesn't have a mane to pad the blow. He yelps and retreats to his proper place. Soon he will need to leave the pride. Male leaders don't like to share their pride with other male lions. The cub will live on his own for a couple years. Then he'll start his own pride with other lionesses somewhere else.

While the lion eats, the females rub their faces together. Scent glands on their faces secrete chemicals that help them recognize one another. Then the grooming begins. The lionesses use their rough tongues to comb out one another's and their cubs' fur.

A lioness cleans her cub.

When the lion has eaten his fill, he stretches out on the grass near the tree. The females and their cubs take their turn eating. Meanwhile, the lion is already back asleep.

Last night for dinner, the lion and his pride ate...

. . . a cheetah cub, snatched while his mom was out hunting. To see what another cheetah is up to, TURN TO PAGE 13.

. . . a gerenuk stretching for some high leaves. To see what another gerenuk is up to, TURN TO PAGE 30.

. . . an olive baboon and her baby. To see what another olive baboon is up to, TURN TO PAGE 24.

. . . a newly born hippopotamus. To see what another hippopotamus is up to, TURN TO PAGE 32.

. . . a dwarf mongoose, digging for its meal. To see what another dwarf mongoose is up to, TURN TO PAGE 40.

. . . a northern white rhinoceros calf that strays too far from its mother. To see what another northern white rhinoceros is up to, TURN TO PAGE 50.

. . . an ostrich chick caught out in the open. To see what another ostrich is up to, TURN TO PAGE 51.

. . . a baby African elephant that got separated from its mother. To see what another African elephant is up to, TURN TO PAGE 54.

CHEETAH
(*Acinonyx jubatus*)

As dawn breaks, the cheetah rises. She stretches her long back and each of her extralong legs. Then she climbs a nearby termite mound to take a look around for **prey**.

There she spies an impala, a kind of antelope. The impala is young and a little too far out on its own. The cheetah lowers her head to stalking position. She creeps forward through the grass until she's about 130 feet (40 meters) away. The impala senses danger and starts to flee. The chase is on. The cheetah's long legs

Leopards and Cheetahs

Like cheetahs, leopards are spotted cats that hunt in the savanna. So what's the difference between these two big cats? Well, a lot. A cheetah is taller, lighter, and faster. It is built to catch prey on the run. Leopards are lower to the ground and more muscular. They use their strength to sneak up on prey and drag it into trees. But if you're going just by looks, it's simple. A cheetah's spots are solid black dots. A leopard's are black circles around a tan spot.

leopard

and back help her. They stretch out so far that she can cover almost 20 feet (6 m) of ground with each running leap. In a flash, she hits her top speed of 70 miles (113 kilometers) per hour. She's going as fast as a car on a highway! She's also faster than any other animal on land.

A cheetah chases down a gazelle.

The impala runs for its life. But the cheetah catches up and swipes out a paw. The impala falls. Before it can rise again, the cheetah clamps down on its neck. The impala's airway is closed off. It dies very quickly. The entire hunt takes less than a minute.

Cheetahs usually live alone. But this is a new mother with cubs. She brings the impala back to her den. When she arrives, her cubs tumble out for breakfast. They are eager to gobble down this meal. But soon the mother cheetah will make them work for their meals. She'll bring her prey back alive and release it. That way her cubs can practice *their* chasing and pouncing.

Cheetahs usually go several days between meals. **But yesterday morning, the cheetah chased down...**

. . . **a spotted hyena cub.**
To see what another
spotted hyena is up to,
TURN TO PAGE 20.

. . . **a Grevy's zebra colt that
dawdled near the water hole.**
To see what another Grevy's
zebra is up to, TURN TO PAGE 23.

. . . **an olive baboon, poking
at an anthill.** To see what
another olive baboon is
up to, TURN TO PAGE 24.

. . . **a blue wildebeest baby.**
To see what another blue
wildebeest is up to, TURN TO
PAGE 26.

. . . **a gerenuk fawn walking
through the long grass.** To
see what another gerenuk
is up to, TURN TO PAGE 30.

. . . **an African wild dog pup in
her den.** To see what another
African wild dog is up to,
TURN TO PAGE 31.

. . . **a dwarf mongoose under
an acacia tree.** To see what
another dwarf mongoose is
up to, TURN TO PAGE 40.

. . . **an ostrich chick,
searching for her first meal.**
To see what another ostrich
is up to, TURN TO PAGE 51.

NILE CROCODILE (*Crocodylus niloticus*)

With a flick of her powerful tail, the Nile crocodile lunges out of the water hole. Snap! The croc clamps her strong jaws on a hartebeest, a kind of antelope, and pulls her **prey** underwater. The poor antelope doesn't know what hit him. Almost immediately other crocodiles circle around, each getting a piece of the hartebeest. They rip and shred him, tipping their heads back as they gulp down chunks. They hardly bother to chew. Their four stomachs will digest even bones and shells.

When there's no trace of the hartebeest left, the crocodile glides back to shore. This time she tromps out of the water. Crocodiles are the only reptiles that lift their bellies off the ground when they walk. That and her webbed feet help her to walk across the muddy shore. She finds a sunny spot and settles in to soak up the warmth.

16

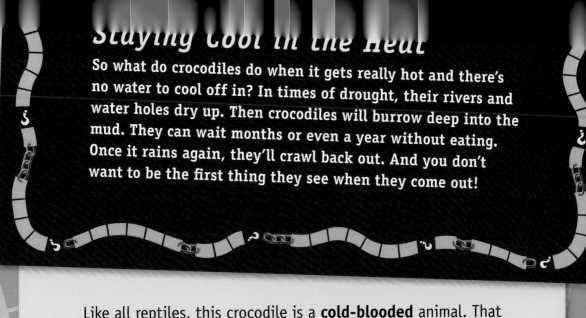

So what do crocodiles do when it gets really hot and there's no water to cool off in? In times of drought, their rivers and water holes dry up. Then crocodiles will burrow deep into the mud. They can wait months or even a year without eating. Once it rains again, they'll crawl back out. And you don't want to be the first thing they see when they come out!

Like all reptiles, this crocodile is a **cold-blooded** animal. That means her body temperature matches the temperature outside. In the savanna, temperatures can be as much as 30°F (17°C) different from morning to night. So she has to soak up all the warmth when she can. When she gets a little too warm, she spreads her jaws wide. The air passing through the inside of her mouth helps her to cool off. Brave thick-knee birds flit in and out of her mouth, snagging bits and pieces of food stuck in her teeth.

This isn't just any place the crocodile has picked to rest. It's the hiding spot for her eggs. She's guarding them from hungry predators. The eggs are carefully tucked away in the sand. She's stayed close by for the last eighty days. In just the past few minutes, they've started squeaking. One baby digs his way out of the sand and then another. They've managed to break their shells with the pointy tips of their snouts, called egg teeth. As the babies grow, they'll lose their egg teeth.

17

The crocodile waits. Then she scoops up two other eggs and rolls them in her mouth. No, she's not eating them. She's cracking the shells and helping those babies hatch. She sets them down near the water and turns back to the nest. Out of the corner of her eye, she sees a raiding lizard. With a growl, she lunges! But it's too late. One of her newborns' tails hangs out the lizard's mouth as he scurries away.

As the rest of the eggs hatch, birds, lizards, and turtles sneak in for a snack. Some of the babies scramble to the water. They are promptly gulped down by giant perch. By midafternoon just two babies remain. They perch on their mother's head, where it's safe. The crocodile will help her young to survive for the next two months. During that time, they'll live off insects, fish, and bigger prey that she catches.

Despite their ferocious reputation as dangerous hunters, crocodiles only eat about once a week. *Last week for dinner, this crocodile snapped up . . .*

A Nile crocodile has its weekly meal—a goose.

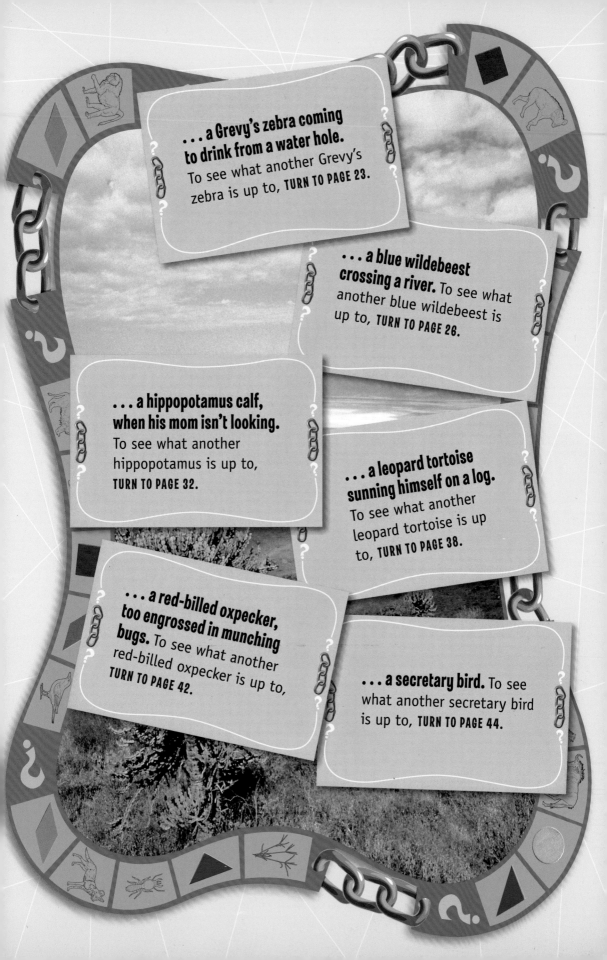

. . . a Grevy's zebra coming to drink from a water hole. To see what another Grevy's zebra is up to, TURN TO PAGE 23.

. . . a blue wildebeest crossing a river. To see what another blue wildebeest is up to, TURN TO PAGE 26.

. . . a hippopotamus calf, when his mom isn't looking. To see what another hippopotamus is up to, TURN TO PAGE 32.

. . . a leopard tortoise sunning himself on a log. To see what another leopard tortoise is up to, TURN TO PAGE 38.

. . . a red-billed oxpecker, too engrossed in munching bugs. To see what another red-billed oxpecker is up to, TURN TO PAGE 42.

. . . a secretary bird. To see what another secretary bird is up to, TURN TO PAGE 44.

SPOTTED HYENA (*Crocuta crocuta*)

The spotted hyena pushes her way through her clan, or family group. The other hyenas are tearing away at a dead Thomson's gazelle they hunted together. But when they see this hyena, they step aside. She is the leader of her clan. That means she gets to eat the clan's catch first.

The hyena rips into the gazelle with sharp teeth. She eats until her tummy sticks out because of all the food. Only then does she step away. As she does, the other females begin to eat. Next will be the cubs. Last will be the clan's males. By the time they eat, all that will be left is bones, hooves, and horns. The males will crunch all that down too.

The lead female trots back to the den, a wide hole dug in the dirt of the savanna. Fifteen hyena babies tumble over one another at the entrance. They aren't all hers. The entire clan's cubs live together in a large den. The lead female's two cubs are the biggest though. They push the others aside, just as their mother did a few minutes ago with the adult hyenas. When her cubs grow up, they'll also be lead females and head clans of their own.

A hyena and her pups leave their den.

Although hyenas hunt larger animals in groups, they often hunt alone. Hyenas are also **scavengers**. Sometimes they'll steal dead **prey** from other predators. *Last night for dinner, the spotted hyena chomped down...*

Strong Stomachs

Hyenas eat just about anything. They'll gulp down any kind of animal, from a live caterpillar to a stinking rotten dead hippo. They'll also swallow any part of an animal. Their strong jaws can crunch through even the toughest horns and bones. Hyenas eat many things that would make other animals very sick or even kill them.

. . . a grazing Grevy's zebra. To see what another Grevy's zebra is up to, TURN TO PAGE 23.

. . . a blue wildebeest calf stolen from a cheetah. To see what another blue wildebeest is up to, TURN TO PAGE 26.

. . . a gerenuk stretching for some leaves. To see what another gerenuk is up to, TURN TO PAGE 30.

. . . a dead African wild dog. To see what another African wild dog is up to, TURN TO PAGE 31.

. . . a hippopotamus calf stuck in the mud. To see what another hippopotamus is up to, TURN TO PAGE 32.

. . . an ostrich chick, feathers, beak, and all. To see what another ostrich is up to, TURN TO PAGE 51.

. . . a dwarf mongoose scratching for some grubs. To see what another dwarf mongoose is up to, TURN TO PAGE 40.

. . . a dead African elephant. To see what another African elephant is up to, TURN TO PAGE 54.

GREVY'S ZEBRA *(Equus grevyi)*

Even though the Grevy's zebra doesn't raise his head, he's already spotted you across the savanna. He can focus on things up close and things far away at the same time. That means he can see both the grass he's eating and a distant predator. Unfortunately, this species' worst predator is often humans. These days very few zebras grace the savannas. They are on the **endangered species list**. That's why this is a *DEAD END*.

Zebra hides are valuable. So is the land the zebras graze on. Cattle farmers want it for their livestock. For these reasons, zebras are being hunted. It has become harder and harder for this species of zebra to survive.

Horses and Zebras

Zebras are closely related to horses, and they look alike in many ways. So, besides the stripes, what are the differences between horses and zebras? Well, zebras are shorter and shaped more like donkeys. They have spikier manes, narrower hooves, and tails with just a tuft of hair at the tip. What's the biggest difference? Humans have been able to tame and train wild horses. But

23

OLIVE BABOON *(Papio anubis)*

High in the jackalberry tree, the olive baboon licks the night's dew off her fur for a quick sip of water. Her troop, or family group, stirs around her. The baboon's baby climbs aboard her stomach for a sort of upside-down piggyback ride. Mother and baby make their way down the tree to the ground with the rest of their troop.

The baboon turns her attention to grooming her baby. With her five humanlike fingers, she flips and combs through his fur. Then the troop lines up in columns behind their male leader. They'll travel 2 to 5 miles (3 to 8 kilometers) today in search of food.

As they hike, the baboon searches for fruit and seeds. A female baboon next to her finds a nest with two eggs. She grabs one and polishes it clean before crunching into it. Our baboon quickly swipes the other. She stashes it in one of her cheek pouches. The other baboon barks a loud complaint. When it comes to food, it's every baboon for herself.

Baboons are **omnivores** and will eat both plants and animals. *Last night for dinner, the baboon tasted...*

Pesky Pests

Most African natives don't consider baboons to be interesting wildlife. While they're fascinating to people outside Africa, they're actually considered pests to many in Africa. That's because in their daily wanderings, baboons often destroy farmers' crops.

. . . a gerenuk calf. Sometimes the baboons will work together to hunt small animals. To see what another gerenuk is up to, **TURN TO PAGE 30.**

. . . secretary bird eggs swiped from a nest. To see what another secretary bird is up to, **TURN TO PAGE 44.**

. . . dung beetle larvae, wriggling in the dirt. To see what another dung beetle is up to, **TURN TO PAGE 46.**

. . . an ostrich egg. Its large size makes it a full meal. To see what another ostrich is up to, **TURN TO PAGE 51.**

. . . acacia tree leaves plucked from the tree. To see what the trees of the savanna are like, **TURN TO PAGE 56.**

. . . a scoop of termites. To see what other termites are up to, **TURN TO PAGE 58.**

BLUE WILDEBEEST *(Connochaetes taurinus)*

Harumph! The blue wildebeest snorts as he yanks up another mouthful of Bermuda grass. This large antelope has a long head with the eyes on top. Those eyes help him to see predators even when he's munching in taller grass.

Not that this guy has anything to worry about at the moment. He's safely tucked away in the midst of his huge herd. Almost a hundred thousand wildebeests are gathered here. Smaller herds are joining in every day. Together, they are migrating, or crossing, the savanna. It's part of a yearly, circular journey.

You think your brothers or sisters crowd you? All wildebeest babies are born within three weeks of one another. That's a lot of cousins and neighbors! In fact, the wildebeests do almost everything together. There's safety in numbers. If the animals are all born near the same time, it's impossible for hungry lions, dogs, or hyenas to eat all of them. And so, most survive.

The wildebeest follows his herd to the banks of a river. The animals stop, nervous at crossing. But soon instincts kick in, and the wildebeests leap into the swirling waters. Our wildebeest paddles across the river as quickly as he can. Many wildebeests will drown in the fast-moving water, but many more will make it across.

Snap! A crocodile lunges out of the water. Will this wildebeest make it?

The crocodile snaps up the unlucky wildebeest to the right. He pulls the creature underwater. Our wildebeest keeps swimming to the other side of the river. The bank is steep and muddy. He staggers past two wildebeests stuck in the mud. Luckily, he finds solid footing.

A hungry Nile crocodile attacks a herd of blue wildebeests.

Magnificent Migration

The Serengeti National Park is one of the most famous savannas in Africa. It is also home to the largest wildebeest migration. Here nearly 1.5 million wildebeests travel in search of food and water. With them are hundreds of thousands of zebras and gazelles. Together these herds travel for much of the year. During that time, they migrate in a circular path that covers about 1,800 miles (2,900 kilometers).

So why migrate if it's so dangerous? During the long dry season, wildebeests must migrate to find enough water and food to survive. Wildebeests are **herbivores**—they feed on the savanna's grasses. When the hot sun dries up the grasses on the plain, the wildebeests must look for food elsewhere. And wildebeests must find rivers and water holes where they can drink. So the herd follows the rain.

Scientists have learned that wildebeests might also migrate in search of natural nutrients called minerals. Certain plants the animals find during their migration may provide them with nutrition that other plants don't.

It's getting dark. The herd slows down for the night. The wildebeest takes his place. He'll sleep lined up with the other wildebeests. That way he'll be protected from the lions and other predators that are just waking up.

Last night for dinner, the wildebeest ripped a mouthful of grass from the trampled ground. Like a cow, he swallowed it whole. Later, he coughed it up as cud and chewed it again.

To learn more about the grass of the savanna, TURN TO PAGE 56.

A herd of wildebeest migrate across a savanna in Kenya.

GERENUK *(Litocranius walleri)*

The gerenuk antelope raises herself on her hind legs like a begging dog. Her front legs pull the river bush willow tree branches down. She stretches out her extralong neck. With this long neck, she reaches leaves too high for other antelope and gazelles. No grass for her. And no water either. She gets all she needs from the leaves on these upper branches. This **herbivore** has found a special spot in the food chain that she perfectly fills.

As the gerenuk eats, she smells the scent of a male gerenuk. He marked this spot earlier as part of his territory. Male gerenuks ooze a black, sticky substance from scent glands near their eyes and knees. This smelly stuff tells other males to stay away. But female gerenuks can pass through in peace.

A few yards off, the grass rustles. The gerenuk buzzes in alarm. It might be a predator after her baby. She's hidden the young gerenuk in a bush not far away. She keeps him clean and even eats his poop so predators can't smell him. But if a hungry predator stumbles across him, his mother cannot defend him. She does not have sharp teeth or claws.

She listens. It's quiet. She hurries over to the bush. When the gerenuk baby sees her, he bleats softly in excitement. He's hungry too and ready to nurse.

Last night for dinner, the gerenuk dined on . . .

. . . **the upper leaves from trees and bushes.** To learn more about trees of the savanna, **TURN TO PAGE 56.**

AFRICAN WILD DOG *(Lycaon pictus)*

See that hole scratched out in the earth near the acacia tree? It's an African wild dog den. Not too long ago, you'd see two or three pups wrestling as they waited for their pack to return from a hunt. But this den, like many others, is empty. In fact, African wild dogs are one of the world's most endangered carnivores. Even though they have been put on

the **endangered species list**, only about three thousand to five thousand are left on the savanna. That makes this a **DEAD END**.

African wild dogs aren't just your neighbor's pets gone wild. They're their own species, distantly related to wolves. But they're finding a hard time staying alive on the savanna. Wild dogs used to tear across thirty-nine countries in Africa. Now they're only spotted in about fifteen. Those fences on the savanna are part of the reason why. Cattle farms have taken over land on the savanna. Fenced-off farmland leaves less room for the dogs to run, hunt, and survive. African dogs also like to hunt cattle. Sometimes cattle ranchers shoot these endangered animals illegally.

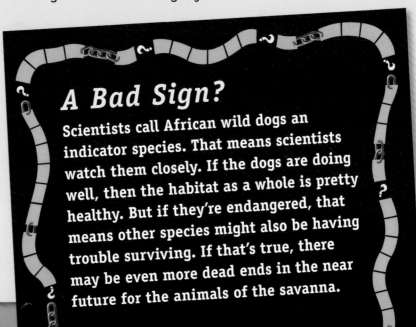

A Bad Sign?

Scientists call African wild dogs an indicator species. That means scientists watch them closely. If the dogs are doing well, then the habitat as a whole is pretty healthy. But if they're endangered, that means other species might also be having trouble surviving. If that's true, there may be even more dead ends in the near future for the animals of the savanna.

HIPPOPOTAMUS *(Hippopotamus amphibius)*

The hippopotamus peers across the water in the river. Just her eyes, ears, and nose are visible above the surface. She's huge and soft looking. But that's not cushy fat. She's almost all muscle and weighs a hefty 3,000 pounds (1,360 kilograms). She's heavy enough to rest on the bottom of the river when she chooses to.

A smaller head pops up next to her. It's the hippo's calf. When he was born, he already weighed 100 pounds (45 kg). These **mammals** spend most of their time in the water. They can even sleep underwater, coming up for breaths without waking up. This little guy wants a drink of his mama's milk. He sinks underwater for a sip. His ears automatically tuck back, and his nostrils seal shut. He can hold his breath for about a minute. His mother can last up to five minutes.

A group of hippos goes for a swim.

A female hippo and her calf at the edge of the water

The hippo herds her calf in closer to shore. It's getting darker, and it's almost time to eat. But she doesn't just plod along through the water. Instead, she performs a slow-motion leap. She pushes off the muddy bottom with her hind legs and glides through the water. She lands lightly on her front legs on the riverbank. Each front foot has four wide webbed toes that steady her.

Behind her, the calf surfaces again. He shakes his head to clear his ears and blows a spray of water from his nose. Suddenly, the water churns white. A crocodile has lunged between the hippo and her baby!

Making Their Own Medicine

If you're brave enough to see a hippo up close, you'll notice something strange. A reddish liquid that's salty, smelly, and oily oozes out of the hippo's pores. No, hippos don't sweat blood. The liquid actually helps protect the hippo from the sun. It also cleans out the animal's wounds. That's right, hippos create their own sunscreen and germ-fighting cream. Scientists are studying it to see if it can someday help humans.

With a bellow, the hippo charges back into the water. Her mouth opens 4 feet (1.2 meters) wide to show 20-inch (51-centimeters) pointy teeth called tusks. She slashes at the crocodile with her head. If she catches the crocodile between her jaws, her thick teeth will easily pierce the crocodile's hide and kill it.

Crocodiles aren't the only ones to be hurt by those tusks. Male hippos use their teeth to fight one another—often to the death. Many surviving hippos are crisscrossed with scars. And for people, hippos are the most dangerous animal in Africa. The large animals kill over three hundred humans a year with those huge teeth.

It doesn't take much to convince the crocodile to give up. It flips its tail and slides out of the way to search for easier **prey**.

With a nudge and a clicking noise, the hippo gets her calf headed to shore. Hippos sound a lot like dolphins and whales. They are closely related to those sea mammals. The calf trots behind her in the twilight. Together they follow a deep rut to their grazing area, a broad field of grass not too far from the river.

This is the same place they go every night. And it's the same food. *Last night for dinner, the hippo chomped...*

...grass. Hippos snip the blades so close to the ground that their feeding area is sometimes called a hippo lawn. To learn more about the grass of the savanna, TURN TO PAGE 56.

A SAVANNA FOOD WEB

Energy moves around the food chain from the sun to plants, from plants to plant eaters, and from animals to the creatures that eat them. Energy also moves from dead animals to the plants and animals that draw nutrients from them.

EGYPTIAN COBRA (*Naja haje*)

In the dark, the Egyptian cobra slithers his 4-foot-long (1.2-meter) body out of the rat's nest. The nest will be his home for a while. The cobra made a meal out of the rat not that long ago.

The snake winds through the brush. He's deaf and has poor eyesight, but he moves with confidence. His tongue flicks out constantly. This action is the reason he knows where he's going. His tongue allows him to taste and smell his way through the world.

The cobra stops. An intruder! He raises his head and spreads the loose skin around his head into a hood. He's warning predators to stay away. But it's just a toad hopping across the path. In a flash, the snake opens his mouth and sinks his fangs into the toad's body.

Venom pumps through the sharp, pointy teeth into the toad. Just a gram (0.04 ounce) of this poison can kill an elephant—or fifty men! The toad doesn't have a chance.

The toad dies quickly. Then the cobra swallows him whole. It'll take the cobra a few days to fully digest his **prey**.

Last week for dinner, the cobra scarfed down . . .

Helpful Uses of Venom

Traditional African medicine uses cobra venom to treat arthritis and rheumatism, two painful diseases. Modern doctors are hoping to develop the venom into a pain reliever drug. It's also being tested as heart medicine and treatment for other diseases. Currently, the venom is most commonly used to make cobra antivenin—a medicine used to treat cobra bites!

. . . another cobra.

. . . a leopard tortoise, shell and all. To see what another leopard tortoise is up to, TURN TO PAGE 38.

. . . a dwarf mongoose, hoping to steal a few cobra eggs. To see what another dwarf mongoose is up to, TURN TO PAGE 40.

. . . red-billed oxpecker eggs. To see what another red-billed oxpecker is up to, TURN TO PAGE 42.

LEOPARD TORTOISE (*Geochelone pardalis*)

The leopard tortoise basks in the sun, soaking up its warmth. But two frisky cheetah cubs dart in and interrupt her.

With her slow walk, she has no chance of outrunning them. Maybe they won't see her. Her yellow and brown spotted carapace, or shell, helps her to blend in with the grass. But no, these playful cubs have caught a glimpse of her and come over to investigate. She does the only thing she can to protect herself. She jerks her limbs and head into her shell. Then she waits.

Leopard Tortoise Eggs

Leopard tortoises lay their eggs in the hard-baked dirt of the savanna. Sometimes the dirt is so hard that a mother tortoise has to urinate to soften it. Then she'll use her back legs to scrape out a nest for the eggs. After they're laid, she'll cover them and then go on her way. Tortoises don't take care of their young. When the baby turtles hatch, they battle the hard, dry soil too. Sometimes they have to wait underground until the rainy season comes. Then they can

The cheetahs sniff the tortoise. They nudge her with their noses. They pat her with their paws. One cub takes a swipe and knocks her over on her back. Eventually, they grow bored and wander off. They weren't hungry so much as just curious. Unfortunately, being upside down is just as dangerous to the tortoise as getting eaten by predators. If she can't flip herself back over, she'll die.

A leopard tortoise protects itself from a lion cub by pulling its limbs and head into its shell.

It's not easy. The sides of her carapace are very steep. Luckily, she's young and hasn't reached her full size. Leopard tortoises can grow to weigh as much as 60 pounds (27 kilograms). The larger a tortoise, the harder it is to knock it over—and the harder it is for it to right itself. Our tortoise uses her strong neck muscles and her claws to rock herself back and forth. Finally, she is able to roll over.

All this work has made her hungry. Leopard tortoises are **herbivores** and live off the grasses and other plants of the savanna.

To read about the grasses of the savanna, TURN TO PAGE 56.

DWARF MONGOOSE *(Helogale parvula)*

The dwarf mongoose pokes his head out of the termite mound he slept in last night. He scampers out into the day. With his foot-long (0.3-meter) body, he's the smallest carnivore on the savanna. Fifteen more mongooses follow him. They squeak to one another as they plan their hunt. The group sticks together. But they don't have a permanent home. They won't return to this mound.

The mongoose scratches furiously in the dirt in search of breakfast. He folds his ears shut to keep out the dust he's slinging. Aha! He finds a trap-door spider hidden under a flap of earth. The mongoose rakes its long claws through the spider's dirt home. Then he gulps down his **prey**.

After that snack, the mongoose teams up with some other mongooses to hunt bigger animals. Together, they rush through the grass. A yellow-billed hornbill swoops over their heads. He often hunts with the mongooses. Their motion through the grass flushes out the insects that the hornbill gobbles up.

Suddenly, the hornbill flaps off. A predator must be nearby! The mongoose rushes to a nearby hollow log and finds a safe hole. Peering out, he glimpses a pack of hyenas passing through. Good thing the hornbill warned the mongooses! Hopefully, the hyenas will leave soon. Our mongoose is still hungry.

Last night for dinner, the mongoose caught...

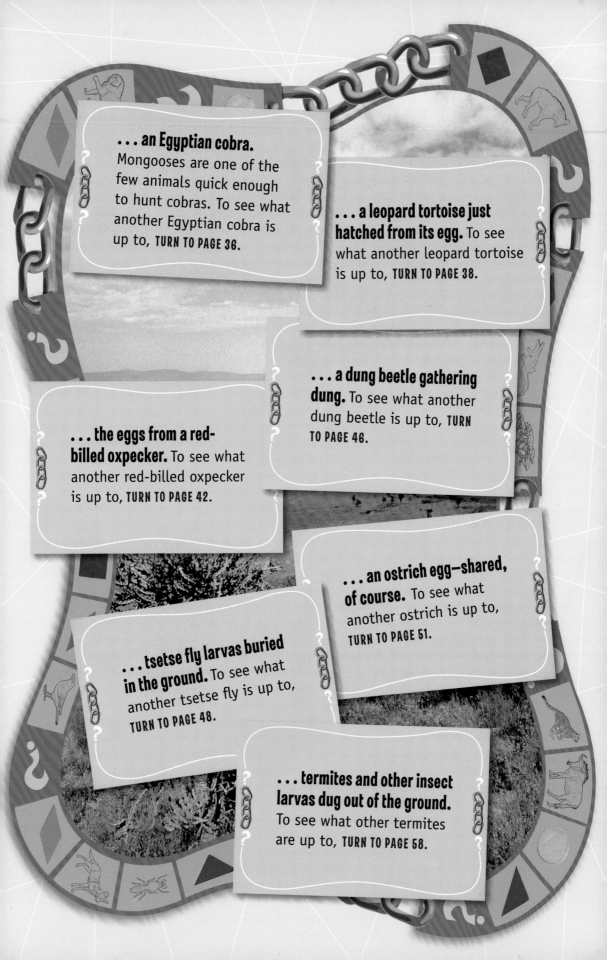

. . . an Egyptian cobra. Mongooses are one of the few animals quick enough to hunt cobras. To see what another Egyptian cobra is up to, TURN TO PAGE 36.

. . . a leopard tortoise just hatched from its egg. To see what another leopard tortoise is up to, TURN TO PAGE 38.

. . . a dung beetle gathering dung. To see what another dung beetle is up to, TURN TO PAGE 46.

. . . the eggs from a red-billed oxpecker. To see what another red-billed oxpecker is up to, TURN TO PAGE 42.

. . . an ostrich egg—shared, of course. To see what another ostrich is up to, TURN TO PAGE 51.

. . . tsetse fly larvas buried in the ground. To see what another tsetse fly is up to, TURN TO PAGE 48.

. . . termites and other insect larvas dug out of the ground. To see what other termites are up to, TURN TO PAGE 58.

RED-BILLED OXPECKER (*Buphagus erythrorhynchus*)

The red-billed oxpecker perches on the side of the African buffalo's face. The bird pecks and plucks at the buffalo's fur with his bright red bill. He hops forward a little and peers in the giant nostril. Then he pokes his head in and pulls out a tick.

The buffalo stomps, shakes his head, and snorts. The oxpecker flies off for a moment before returning. This time he lands on the buffalo's rump. The bird will spend his whole day feasting away on this buffalo's ticks, lice, and flies. Yesterday he rode aboard a rhino. The day before that, it was a giraffe. For the most part, the animals don't mind. They're getting all those itchy pests cleaned off.

42

Red-billed oxpeckers enjoy a meal on the neck of a giraffe.

The oxpecker begins pecking at a wound on the buffalo's side. Oxpeckers mostly help the animals they live off of. But sometimes the birds pick at sores and keep them from healing. That's not good for the animals.

The oxpecker swallows the buffalo's blood. He watches the savanna with his red and yellow eyes. From his perch, he's got a good view. He spots a lion prowling toward them.

The bird chirps and flies off. At this sudden departure, the buffalo raises his head. Then he takes off too. Good thing the oxpecker warned him. The lion is left without a catch.

Last night for dinner, the oxpecker chomped...

. . . blood from a cut on a blue wildebeest's side. To see what another blue wildebeest is up to, TURN TO PAGE 26.

. . . tsetse flies off a hippo's back. To see what other tsetse flies are up to, TURN TO PAGE 48.

. . . ticks from a northern white rhinoceros's body. To see what another northern white rhinoceros is up to, TURN TO PAGE 50.

. . . blood from an African elephant's scrape. To see what another African elephant is up to, TURN TO PAGE 54.

. . . flying termites caught in midair. To see what other termites are up to, TURN TO PAGE 58.

SECRETARY BIRD (*Sagittarius serpentarius*)

The secretary bird strides across the dusty grounds. He's more than 3 feet (1 meter) high, and his long legs look like stilts. The tops of them are covered with black feathers. The bottom half is bare, orange, and bony. Even though he can fly well, he prefers to walk. He's hiked over 10 miles (16 kilometers) so far today.

A whiff of smoke wafts through the air. A grass fire! During the savanna's dry season, fires happen naturally. But this bird doesn't hurry away to safety like the other animals. Instead, he bobs his way toward the fire. He's searching for **prey**, and this is his lucky day. The other animals will be too busy fleeing the fire to notice him.

A poisonous puff adder snake slithers by. The secretary bird steps out to kill it. The puff adder strikes at the secretary bird, but his weaving walk and dipping head makes him hard to catch. Even if the snake did hit the bird, the only part it could reach would be those knobby orange legs. And the skin there is too thick to pierce. The bird raises a foot high and stamps down—right on the snake's skull. He's found his dinner.

But this meal isn't just for him. He scoops up the adder's body and takes off. He'll fly this food back to his mate. The female secretary bird has been sitting on their eggs for the last few weeks.

Last night for dinner, the secretary bird and his mate swallowed . . .

Three's a Crowd

This secretary bird's nest is nearly 8 feet (2.4 m) wide. It's hidden from view at the top of an umbrella thorn acacia tree. His lifelong mate warms the eggs. There are three eggs. When they hatch, probably only two baby birds will get enough food. The third will starve.

... **Nile crocodile eggs and the babies emerging from them.** To see what another Nile crocodile is up to, TURN TO PAGE 16.

... **an Egyptian cobra.** To see what another Egyptian cobra is up to, TURN TO PAGE 36.

... **red-billed oxpecker eggs.** To see what another red-billed oxpecker is up to, TURN TO PAGE 42.

... **a couple of dung beetles.** To see what other dung beetles are up to, TURN TO PAGE 46.

... **some pesky tsetse flies.** To see what other tsetse flies are up to, TURN TO PAGE 48.

... **termites and other insect larva.** To see what other termites are up to, TURN TO PAGE 58.

DUNG BEETLE

(Scarabaeidae)

The two black beetles the size of quarters land on a pile of fresh elephant dung, or poop. They aren't the only ones. Other dung beetles are already swarming the huge stinky pile. But don't worry. There's plenty of dung to go around.

The two beetles are mates. This male and female snack first on the dung. Then they dig with their shovel-shaped heads to carve out a golf ball-sized chunk. To shape it, they walk up and over the chunk of dung. They go around and around, patting it with their front legs. When it's smoothed to their satisfaction, they climb off it and use their stout back legs to push it. Like a snowball, it grows rounder and rounder as they roll it.

They move the ball to their hiding spot, a nice, soft spot on the ground. Once the ball is in place, they start to dig a hole underneath it. The female beetle will lay a single egg in the ball. That way the egg will be safe from hungry predators. When it hatches, the **larva** will feed off the egg.

All animals poop, so there's a lot of food for the beetles to choose from. But in general, the bigger the animal the better. *Last night for dinner, the dung beetles ate . . .*

. . . the dung of a lion. To see what another lion is up to, TURN TO PAGE 8.

. . . the dung of a cheetah. To see what another cheetah is up to, TURN TO PAGE 13.

. . . the dung of a spotted hyena. To see what another spotted hyena is up to, TURN TO PAGE 20.

. . . the dung of an olive baboon. To see what another olive baboon is up to, TURN TO PAGE 24.

. . . the dung of a northern white rhinoceros. To see what another northern white rhinoceros is up to, TURN TO PAGE 50.

. . . the dung of an African elephant. To see what another African elephant is up to, TURN TO PAGE 54.

TSETSE FLY *(Glossina morsitans)*

The tsetse fly flits from animal to animal in the wildebeest herd. It nips a sick, slow-moving wildebeest and sips its blood. This fly may not look like it, but it is one of the most dangerous creatures on the savanna. The tiny tsetse flies spread disease all over Africa.

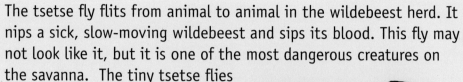

After taking a drink from the sick wildebeest, it darts off to a healthy wildebeest calf. When the fly drinks the calf's blood, it infects the animal with the sick wildebeest's disease. All too soon, the young wildebeest will start to show signs that he's sick too. The disease that tsetse is spreading is called trypanosomiasis. In humans it's known as the sleeping sickness, and it kills thousands of animals and people each year.

Only 5 percent of tsetse flies carry the disease. But there are enough of them that the flies can cause serious damage to herds. A gerenuk on the savanna may get a hundred fly bites a day! So far, researchers haven't found a good solution for the deadly bug. The flies can travel up to 6 miles (9.7 kilometers) a day. So even areas sprayed with bug killer don't stay free of the flies for long.

Last night for dinner, the tsetse fly slurped the blood from . . .

. . . **a Grevy's zebra chewing up some dry grass.** To see what another Grevy's zebra is up to, TURN TO PAGE 23.

. . . **an olive baboon gulping down some fruit.** To see what another olive baboon is up to, TURN TO PAGE 24.

. . . **a blue wildebeest munching on some grass.** To see what another blue wildebeest is up to, TURN TO PAGE 26.

. . . **an African wild dog pup sleeping in its den.** To see what another African wild dog is up to, TURN TO PAGE 31.

. . . **a dwarf mongoose digging in the dirt for food.** To see what another dwarf mongoose is up to, TURN TO PAGE 40.

. . . **a secretary bird hunting for something to eat.** To see what another secretary bird is up to, TURN TO PAGE 44.

. . . **an African elephant.** To see what another African elephant is up to, TURN TO PAGE 54.

. . . **a northern white rhinoceros fighting with its tusks.** To see what another northern white rhinoceros is up to, TURN TO PAGE 50.

NORTHERN WHITE RHINOCEROS
(*Ceratotherium simum*)

The young northern white rhinoceros wanders by, adding to the huge pile of poop that marks his group's territory. He knows that the leader will soon come by. Most likely this adult male will knock over the smelly tower to show that he's boss. But the young rhino is wrong. His group's leader isn't coming by—ever. He was shot two days ago. **Poachers** sawed off his horns to sell and left the rest of his body behind in the grass. Unfortunately, this happens way too often. Because of poachers, rhinos are nearly **extinct** and are on the **endangered species list**. That's why this is a *DEAD END*.

Some people are desperately trying to keep this species alive. Wildlife workers try to catch wild rhinos and give them a drug to put them to sleep. While the rhino sleeps, workers painlessly remove its horns. Rhinos don't need their horns to live, and removing them makes a rhino much less valuable to poachers. People also protect rhinos in zoos and other animal reserves. These animals are carefully watched and taken care of. After all, in many instances, they're the last of their kind.

OSTRICH
(*Struthio camelus*)

The ostrich bends his 9-foot (2.7-meter) frame close to the dust. No, he's not burying his head in the sand. He's stretching out his long featherless neck to gently turn each of the thirty giant eggs in his nest. They're huge! Each one could fit twenty-four chicken eggs inside of it. Moving them every so often keeps the baby ostriches developing right inside their shells.

A female strides up to relieve him. Her feathers are a plain brown compared to his flashy black and white plumes. While all the eggs are his, not all are hers. They're a mix from the five different females he has mated with in their family group. They all live together and take care of the shared nest.

He moves off, fluffing his frothy feathers. The feathers are so graceful and long that they got his ancestors in trouble. In the past, people thought it was fashionable to wear ostrich feathers on their hats and clothes. Ostriches were hunted so much that they almost disappeared. Since then people have worked to prevent ostriches from dying out.

Ostriches are the largest and heaviest birds in the world. They're so large and heavy that they cannot fly. They still move with great speed, though. Ostriches can run 40 miles (65 kilometers) per hour on their strong muscular legs. And their wings? Ostriches stretch their wings out to help them balance and change directions when they run.

The ostrich tosses dirt through his feathers. This dust bath cleans out some of the mites, or tiny bugs, that live there. After his bath, he pecks the ground and gulps down some of the grit and gravel. It's not his meal, but it is necessary for him to eat. He doesn't have teeth, so the gravel inside him will help grind up the food he swallows. And after adding a few pebbles, he's ready to eat.

Ostriches are **omnivores** and will eat both plants and animals. *Last night for dinner, this ostrich gobbled down...*

. . . leaves from a manketti tree. To learn more about trees of the savanna, TURN TO PAGE 56.

. . . leopard tortoise eggs. To see what another leopard tortoise is up to, TURN TO PAGE 38.

. . . a dung beetle, searching for a mate. To see what another dung beetle is up to, TURN TO PAGE 46.

. . . tsetse flies just hatching out of the ground. To see what another tsetse fly is up to, TURN TO PAGE 48.

. . . a couple of termite larvas. To see what other termites are up to, TURN TO PAGE 58.

AFRICAN ELEPHANT *(Loxodonta africana)*

The African elephant slings a spray of mud across her shoulders with her long trunk. The mud coats her skin and protects her from the sun and insects. Her one-year-old baby hangs out in the shade under the elephant's enormous body. Elephants are the world's largest living land animal. Some fully grown males can weigh as much as 13,000 or 14,000 pounds (5,900 to 6,350 kilograms). That's as much as three pickup trucks! However, this elephant is a **DEAD END**. It is in danger of becoming extinct.

In the wild, there are only about three hundred thousand of these elephants left. They're on the **endangered species list**. But **poachers** still shoot elephants and cut off their ivory tusks to sell. This doesn't just kill off the few remaining elephants. It harms elephant families. Older females head elephant families. But hunters kill the oldest elephants first because they have the biggest tusks. Now, younger and younger female elephants have to lead their family groups. Oftentimes they haven't learned all they need to know to do this.

An elephant family walks across a field.

Tusks grow as an elephant ages. The largest elephant tusk collected weighed as much as a grown man—more than 170 pounds (77 kg). But these days, the average tusk comes from much younger elephants. Those tusks are more like the weight of a cat—just 13 pounds (6 kg). If people allowed elephants to die naturally, more than three times as much ivory would be available because the tusks would be so much bigger. But unfortunately, elephants living into old age are getting harder to find.

Elephant's Teeth

Elephant tusks are actually two large teeth. Unlike rhinos and their horns, elephants need their tusks to survive. The animals use them to knock down brush, dig holes, and defend themselves. The rest of their teeth are molars. These flat teeth are used to grind up the 200 to 300 pounds (90 to 136 kg) of plants and grass these herbivores eat each day. Elephants get six sets of twenty-four teeth throughout their lives. As the new ones come in, they push the old ones out the front. The last set comes in when the elephant is thirty years old. They wear out when the elephant is about sixty. After that, an elephant will die of starvation—if he escapes the poachers for that long.

GRASSES, TREES, AND OTHER PRODUCERS

The savanna isn't an easy place for plants to survive. The temperatures are hot during the day and cool at night. And the wet and dry seasons cause floods and droughts. But these producers are as tough as the animals that live here.

Grass carpets the savanna. It's also the center of this habitat's food web. Some grass, such as Bermuda grass, is matted down like a thick carpet. Its deep roots suck up water far below the dry ground. Other grass is tall enough to hide the animals that wander through it. Elephant grass sprouts 10 feet (3 meters) tall. It will slice into your skin with its razor-sharp edges. Where it grows, only the smallest or the thickest-skinned animals can go.

Trees are another important plant on the savanna. They are few and far between, but they offer needed shade and food to many animals. Some trees, such as the river bushwillows, grow near water. Others have small leaves or even no leaves! A tree without leaves can hold water inside its trunk for long periods of drought. Baobab trees are leafless for nine months a year. But because of their ability to store water, they can survive for a thousand years.

Trees and grass are just some of the plants that feed the animals on the savanna. Bushes and leafy plants are other common producers. All of them need nutrients from material such as dead plants and animals that feed the soil. *Last night for dinner, the plants of the savanna soaked up nutrients from...*

sunlight

carbon dioxide

oxygen

Plants make food and oxygen through photosynthesis. Plants draw in carbon dioxide (a gas found in air) and water. Then they use the energy from sunlight to turn the carbon dioxide and water into their food.

. . . poop, spread around by dung beetles. To see what another dung beetle is up to, TURN TO PAGE 46.

. . . a dead spotted hyena. To see what another spotted hyena is up to, TURN TO PAGE 20.

. . . a dead lion. To see what another lion is up to, TURN TO PAGE 8.

. . . a dead cheetah. To see what another cheetah is up to, TURN TO PAGE 13.

. . . a dead Nile crocodile. To see what another Nile crocodile is up to, TURN TO PAGE 16.

. . . a dead hippopotamus. To see what another hippopotamus is up to, TURN TO PAGE 32.

. . . a dead Egyptian cobra. To see what another Egyptian cobra is up to, TURN TO PAGE 36.

. . . a dead secretary bird. To see what another secretary bird is up to, TURN TO PAGE 44.

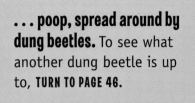

TERMITES, INSECT LARVA, AND OTHER DECOMPOSERS

You can't miss a termite mound. Like a giant mound of clay, it towers higher than your head. Those termites have an important job on the savanna. Along with insect **larva**, they break down the plant matter of the savanna. If they didn't chew logs and leaves into pulp, the savanna would be littered with dead trees and plants.

Other decomposers help to break down the bodies of dead animals. After a lion eats a wildebeest, first **scavengers** such as vultures pick off the remains. Then flies and insect larva start to work on the tiny bits. Their work helps to feed the grass and trees of the savanna.

Last night for dinner, the decomposers feasted on . . .

Termites move in and out of a termite mound.

Vultures feast on a dead animal.

... the fallen branches and leaves of a tree. To learn more about the trees of the savanna, TURN TO PAGE 56.

... a dead lion. To see what another lion is up to, TURN TO PAGE 8.

... a dead cheetah. To see what another cheetah is up to, TURN TO PAGE 13.

... a dead Nile crocodile. To see what another Nile crocodile is up to, TURN TO PAGE 16.

... a dead spotted hyena. To see what another spotted hyena is up to, TURN TO PAGE 20.

... a dead Grevy's zebra. To see what another Grevy's zebra is up to, TURN TO PAGE 23.

... a dead African wild dog. To see what another African wild dog is up to, TURN TO PAGE 31.

... a dead Egyptian cobra. To see what another Egyptian cobra is up to, TURN TO PAGE 36.

GLOSSARY

bacteria: tiny living things made up of only one cell

carnivore: an animal that eats other animals

cold-blooded: using outside energy, such as heat from the sun, to warm body temperature. Reptiles are cold-blooded animals.

decomposers: living things, such as bacteria or fungi, that feed on dead plants and animals

drought: a long period without rain

endangered species list: a list of animals that are in danger of becoming extinct. The lists are usually kept by governments or wildlife agencies.

extinct: no longer existing

food chain: a system in which energy moves from the sun to plants and to animals as each eats and is eaten

food web: many food chains linked together. Food webs show how plants, animals, and other living things are connected in a habitat.

habitat: the place where a plant or animal naturally lives and grows

herbivore: an animal that eats plants

kopjes: stony hills or cliffs in the savanna

larva: the wormlike stage in an insect's life between the egg and adult forms

mammals: animals that have hair and feed their babies milk from their bodies

nutrients: food that helps a plant or animal survive

omnivores: animals that eat both plants and animals

poachers: people who hunt or fish an endangered animal illegally

predators: animals that hunt and kill other animals for food

prey: an animal that is hunted for food by another animal

primary consumers: animals that eat plants

producers: living things that make their own food. Plants are producers. They draw nutrients from soil and use energy from the sun to create their own food from water and carbon dioxide.

scavengers: animals that eat the remains of dead animals

secondary consumers: animals and insects that eat other animals and insects

species: a group of related animals or plants

tertiary consumer: animals that eat other animals and that have few natural enemies

FURTHER READING AND WEBSITES

BOOKS

Allen, Christina M. *Hippos in the Night: Autobiographical Adventures in Africa.* New York: HarperCollins Publishers, 2003. The author tells of her five-week trek through Kenya and Tanzania.

Bash, Barbara. *Tree of Life.* San Francisco: Sierra Club Books for Children, 2002. This book describes a year in the life of a baobab tree on the savanna.

Dunphy, Madeline. *Here Is the African Savanna.* New York: Hyperion, 1999. Dunphy tells a circular story of the landscape and animals of the savanna.

Kurtz, Jane, and Christopher Kurtz. *Water Hole Waiting.* New York: Greenwillow, 2002. A good introduction to African wildlife for younger children, this book features a daylong visit to a watering hole in the savanna.

Markle, Sandy. *Crocodiles.* Minneapolis: Lerner Publications Company, 2004. This book in the Animal Predators series describes crocs and their behavior.

———. *Hyenas.* Minneapolis: Lerner Publications Company, 2005. This book in the Animal Scavengers series details the role hyenas play in African habitats.

———. *Lions.* Minneapolis: Lerner Publications Company, 2005. In this Animal Predators book, Markle describes the social behavior and hunting habits of lions on the African grasslands.

———. *Zebras.* Minneapolis: Lerner Publications Company, 2007. Part of the Animal Prey series, this book looks at the zebra's struggle to survive on the plains of Africa.

Patent, Dorothy Hinshaw. *Life in a Grassland.* Minneapolis: Twenty-First Century Books, 2003. This book looks at the diversity, history, and future of the grasslands (primarily) in the United States.

Toupin, Laurie. *Savannas: Life in the Tropical Grasslands.* New York: Franklin Watts, 2005. Toupin describes the animals and landscapes of the tropical savanna.

WEBSITES

Africam
> http://africam.co.za
> Visitors to this site can view live footage of their favorite African savanna creatures.

African Savanna for Kids
> http://nationalzoo.si.edu/Animals/AfricanSavanna/afsavskids.cfm
> This website from the Smithsonian National Zoological Park features jigsaw puzzles, animal facts, coloring sheets, and more, based on their African Savanna exhibits. There's even a cheetah cam and a naked mole rat cam!

Food Webs: African Grasslands
> http://www.gould.edu.au/foodwebs/africa.htm
> This interactive site helps teach visitors about the food chain of the African savanna.

SELECTED BIBLIOGRAPHY

African Wildlife Foundation. N.d. http://www.awf.org/ (April 20, 2008).

Benders-Hyde, Elizabeth, ed. "African Savanna." *Blue Biomes*. 2000. http://www.blueplanetbiomes.org/african_savanna.htm (April 20, 2008).

Grace, Eric S. *The Nature of Lions: Social Cats of the Savannas*. Buffalo: Firefly Books, 2001.

PBS. "Africa: Explore the Regions; Savanna." *PBS.org*. N.d. http://www.pbs.org/wnet/africa/explore/savanna/savanna_eco.html (April 20, 2008).

———. "The Living Edens: Etosah, the Untamed Wilderness." *PBS.org*. N.d. http://www.pbs.org/edens/etosha/index.htm (April 20, 2008).

Sah, Anup. *The Circle of Life: Wildlife on the African Savannah*. New York: Harry N. Abrams, 2003.

Smithsonian Institute and Friends of the National Zoo. "African Savanna." *Smithsonian National Zoological Park*. N.d. http://nationalzoo.si.edu/Animals/AfricanSavanna/ (April 20, 2008).

United Nations Environment Programme: World Conservation Monitoring Centre. N.d. http://www.unep-wcmc.org/ (April 20, 2008).

University of Michigan Museum of Zoology. *Animal Diversity Web*. N.d. http://animaldiversity.ummz.umich.edu/site/index.html (April 20, 2008).

Williams, J. G., and N. Arlott. *A Field Guide to the Birds of East Africa*. London: Collins, 1980.

INDEX

Photo Acknowledgments

The images in this book are used with the permission of: © Nicholas Parfitt/
Stone/Getty Images, background photographs on pp. 1, 4–5, 6–7, 12, 15, 19,
22, 25, 37, 41, 43, 45, 47, 49, 53, 57, 59; © Bill Hauser/Independent Picture
Service, pp. 5, 56; © Gallo Images-Dave Hamman/Photodisc/Getty Images, p. 8;
© Beverly Joubert/National Geographic/Getty Images, pp. 9, 33, 39; © Wim van
den Heever/Tetra Images/Getty Images, p. 10; © age fotostock/SuperStock,
pp. 11, 14, 30, 31, 44, 51, 52, 58 (bottom); © Gerry Lemmo, pp. 13 (both), 20,
23, 26, 32, 38, 42; © Tom Brakefield/Stockbyte/Getty Images, p. 16; © Anup
Shah/The Image Bank/Getty Images, p. 17; © Richard Du Toit/Minden Pictures/
Getty Images, p. 18; © Suzi Eszterhas/Minden Pictures/Getty Images, pp. 21,
27; © Anup Shah/Photodisc/Getty Images, p. 24; © Daryl Balfour/Gallo Images
ROOTS RF Collection/Getty Images, p. 29; © Chris Johns/National Geographic/
Getty Images, p. 34; © Heinrich van den Berg/Gallo Images/Getty Images,
p. 36; © Wendy Dennis/Visuals Unlimited, p. 40; © Nigel Cattlin/Visuals
Unlimited, pp. 46, 48; © Joe McDonald/Visuals Unlimited, p. 50; © Yoshio
Tomii/SuperStock, p. 54; © Michele Burgess/SuperStock, p. 55; © Dr. C.P.
Hickman/Visuals Unlimited, p. 58 (top). Illustrations for game board and
pieces © Bill Hauser/Independent Picture Service.

Front Cover: © Nicholas Parfitt/Stone/Getty Images (background); © Jonathan
And Angela/Taxi/Getty Images (left); © Mike Hill/Photographer's Choice/Getty
Images (second from left); © Darrell Gulin/Photodisc/Getty Images (second
from right); © Wendy Dennis/Visuals Unlimited (right).

About the Authors

Don and Becky Wojahn are school library media specialists by day and writers
by night. Their natural habitat is the temperate forests of northwestern
Wisconsin, where they share their den with two animal-loving sons and two big
black dogs. The Wojahns' other Follow That Food Chain books include *A Desert
Food Chain*, *A Rain Forest Food Chain*, *A Temperate Forest Food Chain*, *A Tundra
Food Chain*, and *An Australian Outback Food Chain*.